What Bereaved Parents Want You to Know (but may not say)

Kathleen B. Duncan

Photos by Gary Cosby, Jr.

ISBN-13: 978-1517528591
ISBN-10: 1517528593

Published by R & K Publishing
PO Box 3233 Wichita Falls, TX 76301-0233

DEDICATION

To all who have experienced the death of a child,
whether by miscarriage, stillbirth, illness, accident, murder, or suicide.
And to those who love those who have lost a child.

May you find healing and peace.

Contents

Introduction 1

What Bereaved Parents Want You to Know 5

What Parents With a Baby in Heaven Want You to Know 13

What NOT to Say to a Grieving Family..19

Healing..25

While We're Waiting 27

About the Author...31

I lift up my eyes to the hills.
From where does my help come?
My help comes from the LORD,
who made heaven and earth.

Psalm 121:1-2 | ESV

Introduction

On August 13, 2013, I joined a club that I never wanted to join and knew little about. I had become a bereaved parent.

Our twenty-year-old son Andrew had been killed in a car wreck along with four of his friends. They were coming back from a day-long cast party north of Dumas, TX, when the driver ran a stop sign. They were broadsided by an 18-wheeler. Five of the six young people aboard the car where killed, including the driver and our son.

Over the next few days, my husband and I faced tasks and decisions no parent ever wants to face. Buying a casket, cemetery plot and head stone. Planning a funeral. Cleaning out his apartment. Burying our son.

We made it through those early weeks and months following The Accident with the love and support of friends and family, many of whom had no idea how to help us. They tried, but they could not understand all that we were going through.

Shortly after The Accident, a friend introduced me to While We're Waiting, a faith-based support group for bereaved parents. With the aid of this ministry and the grace of God, I have found healing, joy and peace.

The next two years, I wrote about my journey on social media and on my blog, which eventually led to this book which features four articles from my blog. I have received comments from parents around the world telling me how these articles helped them heal. Others thanked me for showing them how to help their friends who were grieving.

It is my prayer that my words give insight to others who wish to help grieving parents. I pray my words are healing and helpful to those who grieve. I pray that they help all who read them.

The LORD is my shepherd; I shall not want.

He makes me lie down in green pastures.
He leads me beside still waters.
He restores my soul.

He leads me in paths of righteousness for his name's sake.

Even though I walk through the valley of the shadow of death,
I will fear no evil, for you are with me;
your rod and your staff, they comfort me.

You prepare a table before me
in the presence of my enemies;
you anoint my head with oil; my cup overflows.

Surely goodness and mercy shall follow me
all the days of my life,
and I shall dwell in the house of the LORD forever.

Psalm 23 | ESV

Bereaved[1]

adjective
1. (of a person) greatly saddened at being deprived by death of a loved one.

noun
2. a bereaved person or persons (usually preceded by the): to extend condolences to the bereaved.

Grief

noun
1. keen mental suffering or distress over affliction or loss; sharp sorrow; painful regret.

2. a cause or occasion of keen distress or sorrow.

Note: 1. From http://dictionary.reference.com/

For you formed my inward parts;
you knitted me together in my mother's womb.

I praise you, for I am fearfully and wonderfully made.

Wonderful are your works;
my soul knows it very well.

My frame was not hidden from you,
when I was being made in secret,
intricately woven in the depths of the earth.

Your eyes saw my unformed substance;
in your book were written, every one of them,
the days that were formed for me,
when as yet there was none of them.

Psalm 139: 13-16 | ESV

What Bereaved Parents Want You to Know
(but may not say)

People of faith who have lost a child are often seen as brave and strong. We have been through something that no parent wants to experience: the death of a child.

We are not strong or brave. We endure because we must; we have no choice. We have other family members that need us. We have "good works which God prepared in advance for us to do". We have jobs and homes to care for. We cannot just give up, find a hole to crawl in and quit living -- though we sometimes wish we could.

We are walking through life because that is what we do – we go on. We live. We breathe. We work. And we attend church and school functions because we must. We know that God called our child Home and left us here on earth for His purpose. We know we must persevere and trust Him to help us and to heal us. We do not go on because we are tough or brave or strong. The truth is that we are none of those things. We are most often weak, tired and broken.

Our reality is often different than what we show our friends, our coworkers and the public around us.

We rarely show others the true depth of our pain. It is too personal and too raw to show others who have not experienced it themselves; we know that people cannot understand the sorrow of losing a child unless they have walked this path. And we hope and pray that none of our friends ever go through what we have experienced.

The truth is that if someone you love has buried their child, they probably won't be completely open about what they're going through because they're trying so hard to just function and hold it together.

They are trying not to "lose it" in front of you.

We know how uncomfortable our pain is to others. It is a reminder that you, too, could lose a child in an accident or to an illness. It could be your child in the wrong place/wrong time or in the wrong relationship resulting in his or her death. Our pain reminds you that you could someday bury your child.

We know that our pain also makes you feel helpless – there is nothing that you or anyone else can do to change our situation. Our child is gone. We will not see him again until our great reunion in Heaven.

For some, it reminds you that you have also lost a friend, a student, or coworker. It brings up your own pain and grief when you see us cry or see the sorrow in our eyes. We don't want to cause you that pain or make you uncomfortable with our grief.

We also don't want to "lose it" because it is so hard to get control once the tears start flowing.

At first, the tears of a bereaved parent are not "healing tears". They are tears of a deep, intense sorrow like none other. They are exhausting and embarrassing. We have had friends try to comfort us and tell us it will be okay. It will not be okay! Our child is dead! As time goes on, and if we do the right kinds of "soul care" to help us heal, the tears change to healing tears. But it takes a long time.

We are afraid, sometimes, that if the tears start, they won't stop. So we try hard not to let them start.

The tears remind us of that horrible physical grief-pain that lasted so long. We are reminded of waking up to realize this is not some terrible nightmare. It is our reality now. We are bereaved parents.

So we hide our pain.

We smile and laugh and go on living. We thank you when you tell us again how sorry you are and how much you miss our kid. We tell you we are doing well and that God is good.

God is good. He is faithful. He is healing our broken hearts. We do have joy and peace. We do have moments of happiness and fun-filled laughter. We will recover. We will be healed and go on living. But our life has changed and we will never be quite the same as we were before burying our child.

As a result, bereaved parents aren't completely honest with you. However, if we could be truly honest and vulnerable, we would tell you:

1. **Don't wait for me to call you.** Please call me every once in a while. I know you told me to call if I ever needed anything, but it's hard to call and ask when I am hurting so badly. I don't want to appear weak. Or pathetic. I don't seem to have the strength to ask anyone to do things with me. Sometimes just returning a text is too hard. I need you to keep trying, to keep calling. Call with a specific plan like "can you go to lunch at 11:30 next Tuesday?" not just "let's have lunch sometime".

I *will* get better and want to go with you to that dinner, movie or play some day. And if I say "no thanks" this time, I need you to ask again. I need you to call me just to chat, even when I may not feel like chatting. I need you to call me to help me remember that the world continues to turn and life goes on and that you want me to be a part of it.

2. **Listen. Really listen.** Please don't assume that because you read my blog or Facebook posts that you know how I feel. I don't even know how I feel sometimes! And I am not completely honest on Facebook; no one is. I may appear to be doing really well based on social media when, in reality, I am struggling. I need friends who are willing to listen to me without correction or platitudes. Listen as I talk about my kid, yet again. I will thank

you for taking time to listen to me. I will appreciate your patience and caring enough to listen when I need to talk. And I will try to listen to you when you are in need.

3. **Don't assume my tears are because of grief.** Even though the loss of a child is not something we just get over, grief is not always what is bothering me. I may be having an off day because I feel ill, or because I had a disagreement with my spouse or because we are having trouble with one of our other children. Don't assume that my issues or prayer requests are always because I buried my son. Ask me. I need you to let me have emotions and experiences that have little or nothing to do with grief. And please don't tell me it's going to be okay. Let me be honest with you about my emotions without trying to fix them.

4. **Don't ask me about how I feel.** That is a very hard question to answer honestly. Some days are good, some are bad. Some moments are good and the next may be terrible. Ask me what I have been doing lately or what plans I have for the upcoming week. Ask me what I am studying or what my kids are doing. Ask me almost anything, but please don't ask me how I feel.

5. **Be patient with me and forgive me when I am rude or short with you.** The death of a child changes one in ways you cannot imagine. And one does not "get over it". Not in six months, not in a year, not ever. For some, the grief lasts a very long time. Our child is frequently on our minds. We may forget for a little while, but even small things can remind us that they are gone. If I snap at you, ignore you or seem unhappy, please give me some grace. It is most likely not about you at all.

6. **Forgive me if I am not interested in small talk.** Losing a child changes our perspective regarding what is important. We don't seem to care about trivial things anymore. I really do want to listen to you and care about those things that matter to you. But sometimes I just don't see the point of talking about stuff I can't do anything about. My perspective has changed; time is short. I want to care about what the Father cares about. I want to care about and think about eternal things.

7. **Forgive me if I am forgetful.** Grief often causes what is called Grief Brain. If I forget a date or a meeting, forgive me. And know that I am doing my best. If I am supposed to be at something important, you may want to send me a text reminder. I will appreciate the help.

8. **Know that I will forgive you**. Don't avoid me because you don't know what to say. I will try to give you grace when you say hurtful things, because you will. We all do. We don't know what to say around bereaved parents. That's okay. I will be glad you have taken time to be with me and that you tried.

9. **Talk about my child**. And let me talk about him. He was a huge part of my life. He still is. It helps to talk about him. And I love that you have stories to tell me that I did not know! If I begin to tear up, know that you did not cause my pain. My child's death caused my pain. I will pull it together after a few tears or I will excuse myself and find a place for a good cry. It really is healing to know that others care about and miss my child.

10. **Don't talk about my child.** There are times when I just need to talk about something else. I want to hear about your family, your children, your life. I want to talk about that new study I am doing or the trip we have planned.

How do you know whether to talk or not talk about my child? Listen for clues: if I ask you about your family, talk about that. If I am especially quiet, ask if I want to talk about him or ask me what I would like to talk about. (And know that I don't always know what I want.) When at social events, I sometimes just enjoy listening to others talk. Don't try to make me join in; let me have some room to just listen.

11. **Give me time.** Grief does not have a timetable. The loss of child is something I will be dealing with the rest of my life. I know that God is good, faithful, kind, compassionate and loving. I know that He will help me through this. But I need time. Some of us heal quickly, some take longer. Some days the burden is light; other days it is unbearable. Please ask me to participate in activities with you, but understand that when I say no, it is not about you. It may just be the grief. It may just be too hard for me right then. But please ask again. And again.

12. **Church is particularly difficult**. We may not know why, but we tend to get emotional at church. Even those of us who never cried at church before often cry now. It is not that we are sad in church. It is just that being in worship, singing and being in His presence bring the emotions to the

surface. For us, the reality of Heaven, Hell and life after death is more pronounced. We are often overwhelmed by God's love and greatness. By His omnipotence. By His grace and love that caused Him to send His only Son to die for me. The reality of all of this is so...well, REAL!

If we cry at church, don't try to comfort us and tell us it's going to be okay or that you understand. Just let us cry. Offer a tissue and maybe a gentle hug. Allow us to worship, even through our tears. If a bereaved parent attends church alone, ask if you may sit by her. And just be near. Or better yet, offer to pick her up and let her ride with you. After service, don't make light of our messed up makeup or runny nose. Give us a few moments to pull ourselves together. Again, a gentle hug and an "I love you" or "I'm sorry you are hurting. I miss him, too" goes a long way.

13. **My kids are hurting.** They lost their brother, their friend. They may not show it, but they are hurting. They don't want to be known as "the dead kid's sister" or "the one whose brother died". They are still who they were before with the same interests and talents. They still need to be with friends and enjoy life apart from their grief. They don't want to talk about their sibling or his death and don't want you to bring it up. Except when they want you to talk about him or bring it up. Be patient with them. See items 1-12.

14. **Dads hurt as much as moms; they just don't often show it.** See items 1-12. It seemed that many of my girlfriends checked in with me that first year. They asked how I was doing. Friends called and texted me to let me know they cared. Not as many friends contacted my husband. Maybe guys just don't think it matters. It does. A few close friends do text him regularly even now to just say, "I am thinking about you. How can I pray specifically for you today?" Knowing that godly men were praying for him and knowing that he had friends to call on helped my husband heal.

15. **God is still on the throne.** Though our child has died, we still know that God is God. Or maybe because we have experienced this life-changing event, we believe more strongly in the sovereignty of God. We know we are not in control; God is. Our faith may be tested, but we choose to believe. And because of our faith, we will be able to go on living.

I would add, "Choose Life!"

One thing I have heard myself saying to my husband recently is that I want to live until I die. I don't want grief to paralyze me. I don't want it to define me. It has changed me, but I don't want it to stop me from living a full and joyful life.

The death of my son has made me realize how precious life is and how it can be gone in a moment. I want my friends to see how precious their children are. I want young people to stop making stupid choices. I want those I love to live a full and Spirit-filled life! I want you to know the Creator and to know that He loves you! Even when ugly things happen - and they will happen - God is beautiful and caring and loving and compassionate and gracious!

So choose Life!

Christ said, "I am the Way, and the Truth, and the Life".

Choose Christ and all that He is and all that He has to give!

Live well, my friends. Live well.

But we do not want you to be uninformed, brothers, about those who are asleep, that you may not grieve as others do who have no hope.

For since we believe that Jesus died and rose again, even so, through Jesus, God will bring with him those who have fallen asleep. For this we declare to you by a word from the Lord, that we who are alive, who are left until the coming of the Lord, will not precede those who have fallen asleep. For the Lord himself will descend from Heaven with a cry of command, with the voice of an archangel, and with the sound of the trumpet of God. And the dead in Christ will rise first. Then we who are alive, who are left, will be caught up together with them in the clouds to meet the Lord in the air, and so we will always be with the Lord. Therefore encourage one another with these words.

1 Thessalonians 4:13-18 | ESV

What Parents With a Baby in Heaven
Want You to Know
(but may not say)

This article addresses some issues which are specific to those who have lost a baby to miscarriage or stillbirth and those whose baby died shortly after birth, possibly due to premature birth or other health issues. Each baby is unique. Each loss is unique. Each person's grief is unique, but all these parents have experienced a special kind of loss.

Many of these parents do not have pictures of their baby - she was born straight into the arms of Jesus before any pictures could be taken. Their baby may not have even had a name; they never knew its gender.

Others have pictures they do not share - their child was born "asleep" and the pictures are not sweet to anyone but his parents.

Some have only a few pictures, and they would love for you to ooh and ahh over them!

Still others have a lock of hair, footprints and a few precious tiny outfits that were never worn.

For some, their memories are of the excitement of finding out they were expecting, followed only by the grief of knowing loss.

Some have fond memories of feeling their little one kick and move...and then stillness. Just stillness. And the pain of loss.

Some did not even know they were expecting until they learned there would be no sweet baby to hold this time.

For some, there were the joys of a full-term baby, only to learn that their baby will not go home and learn to crawl, walk, talk or ride a bike. Because she did not live past birth.

Some got to hold their child and enjoy her for but a few hours or days. She stayed in the hospital her entire life battling just to breathe. And then they buried her.

However long their baby lived, that life is precious to her parents. They are grieving the loss of a child. Some parents have two or three or more babies in Heaven. Each was precious. Each is missed. Each parent grieves in his unique way. They need you to understand some things about their loss, their grief and their healing. Although not all of these apply to every parent, it is helpful for you to understand them.

If you took time to listen - to really listen - without judgement or platitudes or advice, this is what bereaved parents of infants might say to you.

1. **Though my child lived for a short time, she is real.** She lived. She lives now in Heaven. I am a parent. You may have a child who lives in Toledo; mine lives in Heaven.

2. **Please do not tell me I will have other children**. Only God knows if I will ever have another child. And by saying that, you have just brought up one of my biggest fears: that I will never have another child. In addition, you have minimized the value of this child! She is valuable to me and to her dad. And to God. And please don't ask me if we plan to "try again". I am still healing from this loss. When, and if, we decide to "try again", it will be a private decision between us and God.

14

3. **Please don't tell me it was the will of God, or she's in a better a place, or it was for the best**. I know that the Lord gives and the Lord takes away. I know that Heaven is a beautiful place. I know that God knows what is best for me and for my child. But none of that helps me right now.

4. **And please don't tell me that God needed another angel in Heaven**. Statements like this do not help me. The God I serve does not need anything. He is God all by Himself. He is kind and loving and gracious and compassionate and wise. He would not take my baby because He needed another angel. He created my child. He wove her together in my womb, and He knew every one of her days before one of them came to be. I don't know why my child died, but I know that He created her and He loves her, and right now, that has to be enough.

5. **If you must speak, tell me you are sorry for our pain and that you love us.** Tell us that you will pray for us. And ask us what we need; ask how you can help us today.

6. **I may not have pictures of him, but I knew him**. I had dreams of what he would look like, how he would feel in my arms, and of caring for him. I talked to him and thought about him as he moved in my womb. I knew him -- and I loved him. I still love him.

7. **His daddy loves him, too**. My husband is hurting. He had dreams of being a daddy to our baby. Plus he has seen his wife go through a physically difficult event. He is hurting over the loss of our child, and he is hurting because he loves me and sees me hurting. I am hurting to see him hurting. We are both hurting. We need healing. Please pray for us both.

8. **How we memorialize our baby and honor her life is our choice.** Please don't tell me it is foolish to spend all that money on burying my child. Or that I should have had a ceremony when we chose not to. This is our child, our grief, our decision. Our family is doing what we need to do to heal. If we invite you to a memorial, please come! We want you there to celebrate our child's life and to mourn with us. If we have private ceremony, please do not be offended. We needed to be alone with her just one more time. If we do not have a service, that was our decision to make.

9. **Our other children are hurting and need time to grieve.** Please be considerate of what you say to them. If you would not say it to me, don't say it to them. If you are not willing to ask me, don't ask them. They were excited about the new baby. They may have questions - answer them if you

must, but we prefer that you direct them to talk to us about this loss. If our children are young, they may not understand much; please don't try to explain things to them - that is our job. If our children are older, they understand more, and hurt more because they understand more.

10. **I need time to heal physically.** Even if I do not recognize it, my body needs time to heal. Not only have I been through a difficult physical event, I am exhausted from grief. I find it hard to clean, cook, or do laundry. I am tired. Please allow me to heal physically. Don't expect me back at my volunteer position at church or out on the jogging track right away. Let me have time to heal.

11. **Your offer of a meal is appreciated.** But please don't plan on staying and chatting when you drop off dinner next Tuesday. If I ask you in, please stay for just a little while. I am not up to chatting or putting on a happy face. Not yet. And don't be offended if I don't come to the door, I may be resting. Or crying. Other ways you could love us include cleaning, rides to doctor appointments, groceries, and hand written cards. My family appreciates that you care enough to help us during our time of grief.

12. **Please don't tell me your horror miscarriage story!** I am sorry that you, too, know the pain of loss. But your horror story does not help me. Maybe someday, when I have time to mourn my child and time for my heart to heal, we can find time to get together. It may be helpful to me to hear your story of loss and healing. But it will not be helpful for me to hear horror stories. Ever.

13. **I am glad for you that you are having a baby.** But your pregnancy reminds me of my loss. If I don't come to your shower, please don't take it personally. I am hurting still. I don't want to cry and take away from your joy. I am so glad you invited me, but I need more time.

14. **I rejoice with you in the birth of your happy, healthy baby.** But my arms are empty. And holding your child only makes it worse. Please don't offer for me to hold him in front of others. Could we find a time alone, in

a safe place for me to meet your child? Some place where I can cry while rejoicing with you over how perfect his little toes are? I really am healing. I want to celebrate with you. I just can't do it publicly, not yet anyway.

15. **Each of us grieves in our own way**. For some, this is a huge life-altering event. They may take a long to heal from their grief. Others heal more quickly. Please let me grieve my way, even if it is different than the way you grieved - even if it is different than you expected.

Not all of these will apply to every bereaved parent.

Ask me what I need. And know that I will heal. I will recover. I will be happy again. Someday. With God's help. Thank you for allowing us to grieve in the best way we know how. Thank you for loving us in our grief. Thank you for praying for us as we heal. Thank you for acknowledging that our baby lived and that we are grieving his death.

For everything there is a season,
and a time for every matter under heaven:
a time to be born, and a time to die;
a time to plant, and a time to pluck up what is planted;
a time to kill, and a time to heal;
a time to break down, and a time to build up;
a time to weep, and a time to laugh;
a time to mourn, and a time to dance...

Ecclesiastes 3:1-4 | ESV

What NOT to Say to a Grieving Family

When we see someone hurting, we all want to say something, anything, to make it better. The truth is, for a grieving family, you cannot make it better with your words. And some things you might say can actually make a grieving parent feel worse.

Only God can heal the brokenness felt by a parent who has buried their child.

Here is a list of things not to say to a grieving family. If you do say one of these things, know that we will forgive you. We know you are trying to help and love us. We are thankful for that. We try to walk in grace and forgiveness. However, if you can, take time to think before you speak. And please try not to say these things to a grieving mother or father.

1. **I know what you're going through**. Unless you have walked in their shoes, you cannot know all that another person is facing. You cannot know their fears, pain and struggles.

Unless you have lost a child, you cannot know what a bereaved parent is going through. It sometimes feels as if you are minimizing my pain when you compare what I am going through with your own loss. The loss of a pet, friend, job, or parent does not compare to the loss of a child. Please don't try to compare them. Instead, try saying, "I am sorry you are going through this."

2. **I understand your pain.** Unless you have lost a child, you cannot possibly understand the pain of bereaved parents. Even if you have experienced a deep loss yourself, your loss was different than mine. Each of us is unique. Our children were unique. Their deaths were unique. And our grief is unique. A better thing to say might be, "I understand that you are hurting. I am sorry."

3. **How are you doing? Or How are you feeling?** Only ask this if you have the time to really listen. And please don't try to get us to *really* tell you how we are unless we are close friends. Only ask if we are in a private place. If we open up to tell you how we are really doing, it may get ugly. Grief can be ugly. Tears and snot and stuff. Honestly sharing how I am may not be easy for you or me. Please know that this road is hard. It is harder than you could ever imagine. We have good moments and bad moments. We will survive, but talking about the hard stuff is…well…hard. Maybe you could ask, "How is your week going" or "What do you have planned this weekend?"

4. **God always picks his best flowers first.** Statements like this are theologically wrong at best; at worst, they are hurtful. You have just told a grieving momma that God "picked" her son to be killed by that truck or to die of that rare cancer because their child was such a good flower. This is not helpful.

I had a friend tell me just two months after The Accident, "You may not be ready to hear this, but God killed your son." No, I was not ready to hear that. I don't think I will ever be ready to hear that.

There is scriptural foundation to say that God chose and knew their child and that He controls the number of our days, but to tell a grieving parent that God picked their child to die because they were so wonderful is completely unhelpful.

Again, try sticking with, "I am sorry you are going through this."

5. **God must have needed another angel in Heaven.** God does not need anything. He is God all by himself. He did not take my son because He needed an angel. If God needed another angel, he could have spoken a word and one would be created.

Angels are created beings, different from humans who were formed in the image of God. It's okay to refer to our children as angels, but please don't tell a grieving parent that God took their child because he needed an angel. Perhaps you could stick with, "I am sorry. It must be so hard to lose a child."

6. **She's in a better place.** Yes, Heaven is a wonderful place; however, knowing Heaven is wonderful does not make us hurt any less. Knowing truth does not take away the pain or sorrow. Platitudes do not fix our grief. We miss our son. We always will. Knowing he is in Heaven does not change that for parents. It might be best to validate our feelings and express

your condolences. Again, try sticking with, "I am sorry you are going through this."

7. **At least you can have another child.** You do not know that. No one knows that. Only God knows if they can have more children.

A friend told me after a miscarriage, "When people say things like that, they have just brought up one of my worst fears: that I may not be able to have another child. It brings up my pain and fear."

Even if we do have more children or adopt, those children will never replace the one that died. That child is special to us. He was loved and wanted. This kind of statement diminishes his importance. Please acknowledge our loss and our pain. Acknowledge that this child was special to us and can never be replaced. A better thing to say to a momma who has lost a child is, "I am sorry for your pain. I am sorry you are going through this."

8. **It's a good thing you have other children.** Yes, my other children are a blessing. They love me and I love them. They helped me heal. But none of them was Andrew. They are each unique. Having other children does not fill the void left by the death of our son. It is better to acknowledge our loss. Acknowledge that we will miss our son. A better thing to say would be, "I am sorry for your pain."

9. **If you had just had more faith, this might not have happened, or your child might have been healed, or whatever.** There are many instances in the Bible of Jesus healing people who had great faith and of Jesus healing those who had no faith. And there are those who had great faith but still suffered. Jesus suffered. Paul Suffered. David Suffered. Moses suffered. My child did not die because of my lack of faith.

This statement feels like you are judging my faith, like you are saying it is my fault my child is dead. And that is very hurtful. Please do not ever say this to a family who has just buried a loved one. Sometimes it's best to just say, "I am sorry for your pain. I am sorry you are going through this."

10. **God must be trying to teach you something.** The truth is that God is always teaching us, but saying this to a grieving parent is hurtful. This statement is saying that God killed my child to teach me something. Do you want to serve a god that would kill your child to teach you something? I don't.

Yes, God will use this. I will grow and learn. God will use all things in my life for my good and His glory. But, sometimes it's best to just say, "I am sorry for your pain. I am sorry you are going through this."

11. **God will never give you more than you can handle.** God often gives us more than we can handle. He does want us to rely on Him. He promises to never leave us or forsake. He promises to always be with us. He promises to love us. But He never promises to give us only what we can handle.

He will walk with grieving parents and He will help them through this horrible grief, but the death of a child is absolutely more than any of us can handle without His help. Perhaps this would be better -- "I am sorry you are going through this. I pray that God will give you comfort."

12. **You're so strong. I could never be as strong as you.** To some, this implies that we are facing the death of our child because of our strength. As if, well… if we were not so strong then we would not be going through this. Like it is *my fault* for being so strong.

This statement also makes it difficult for us to be weak. It may feel like others are expecting us to be strong all the time. As if they expect us to be super-human or super Christians. Please let us be weak. Let us be human. Let us grieve.

If you had asked me a day before The Accident what would I do if my child was killed, I would have told you that I would curl up in corner and want to die myself. However, I have gained strength through Christ as I have walked this path. He has strengthened me through His Spirit in my inner being so that Christ can dwell in my heart through faith. And my faith is the gift of God, it is not my own doing.

Some days I am still weak. I still grieve. I still cry. I still have bad days. I am grateful that God gives us strength to walk the road He has set before us. Rather than telling a parent how strong she is, try saying, "I am sorry you are going through this."

What should you say?

The morning after The Accident, our dear friend Jeff appeared at our door. He arrived within an hour of us learning of our son's death and posting it on social media. (That was the only way we knew to let Andrew's friends know what happened.) Jeff had clearly been crying. He came in, wrapped his arms around Ron and me and said, "There are no words. I am sorry. I love you."

This is exactly what you should say to a grieving parent:

There are no words.
I am sorry you are going through this.
I love you.

Blessed be the God and Father of our Lord Jesus Christ, the Father of mercies and God of all comfort, who comforts us in all our affliction, so that we may be able to comfort those who are in any affliction, with the comfort with which we ourselves are comforted by God. For as we share abundantly in Christ's sufferings, so through Christ we share abundantly in comfort too. If we are afflicted, it is for your comfort and salvation; and if we are comforted, it is for your comfort, which you experience when you patiently endure the same sufferings that we suffer. Our hope for you is unshaken, for we know that as you share in our sufferings, you will also share in our comfort.

2 Corinthians 1:3-4 | ESV

Healing

As I look back over those first two years – reading posts, blog articles and my personal notes – I am struck by how raw my wound was and how excruciating daily living was. I see the pain, the sorrow and intense grief I experienced in those first months. I see how simple tasks were extremely difficult. I remember how hard it was dealing with the paperwork and the decisions we had to make. And I am in awe that I no longer walk in that pain. I no longer walk in a fog of constant sorrow and grief.

There is a void in my life that only Andrew filled. I miss his laugh, his stomping through the house, his hugs and his stories. Nothing will ever replace my son in my life. I still have moments and even days of sadness. Some memories still bring tears. I see his friends dance, graduate, get new jobs or get married and these things bring a twinge of regret that I don't get to see Andrew do those things. I hate that his nephews won't know him like they will know their other uncles and aunts. Yes, I will grieve my son until I die.

However, those early days of sorrow so deep that I physically ached are gone. The days of doubt, sobbing and aching have passed. Seeing an old picture of all four of my boys together no longer takes my breath away. I no longer count the days, weeks, or months since I saw him last or since the date of his death. I no longer cry each time I see a picture of him or hear his name. I no longer wake up with my pillow wet from my tears. Death is no longer a central theme in my thoughts.

Pictures and stories of my son bring a smile. I enjoy looking back at his Facebook, seeing photos of him with his friends and hearing stories of their antics. I rejoice at seeing his friends growing and living. I know that they were changed for the better by having Andrew in their lives, and I know that they have not forgotten him.

Friends, family and, of course, grandchildren bring me joy. I have peace. I sleep well. Sometimes I dream of Andrew, and I am glad. I ride my bike, travel with Ron and mow my property. I read great books, study my Bible and enjoy movies and TV. I play with my dogs, visit with friends and go out to eat. In short, I live.

I know I have forgotten things about Andrew, stories he told, little things. I see pictures and wish he were here to tell me the backstory. I miss Andrew. I know my son lived. He lived well. He still lives.

My heart is no longer broken. I no longer ache all over. I no longer think of death, dying, grief and pain much of the time. Yes, there is a void. Yes, there is a scar. Yes, I have experienced loss. But in Christ I have found peace, joy and strength to go forth and do the next right thing.

This is what I mean when I say my broken, shattered heart has been healed by a loving, gracious, living God. When I say that I have found healing after The Accident, I don't mean that I no longer grieve.

As you try to comfort a mother or father who has experienced the death of a child – a child of any age and by any cause - remember that they will grieve their child forever. Or at least until we join them in Heaven. Please know that their birthday and the date of their death will always be difficult days. Even when it doesn't look like they still grieve, please know that they miss their child.

Mention our children. Share your memories. Acknowledge our pain. And pray for us. Pray that we find joy. Pray that we have happy memories. Pray that we find healing in a loving, living God.

While We're Waiting

Less than a month after our son died, a friend introduced me to a faith-based ministry called While We're Waiting. The parents in this group have all experienced the death of a child. Over the next two years, these parents helped me heal. They listened, they prayed, they encouraged and they shared their own stories of loss, grief and healing. If you have lost a child, I encourage you to look into this amazing ministry.

Facts about the While We're Waiting Ministry

While We're Waiting was co-founded in April of 2011 by Brad and Jill Sullivan, whose 17 year old daughter, Hannah, went to Heaven in February of 2009 after a year-long battle with brain cancer, and Larry and Janice Brown, whose 36 year old son, Adam, a member of Navy SEAL Team SIX, went to Heaven in March of 2010 when he was killed in Afghanistan. Board members include Tiffany McCain, whose daughter, Lily, was stillborn in 2008, and Charles & Christy Swain, whose 17 year old son, Ryan, drowned in 2013.

The mission of While We're Waiting is to bring bereaved parents together in order to provide a faith-based network of encouragement and support as they grieve the loss of their children. Our goal is always to point grieving parents to our only true source of comfort, Jesus Christ. Our desire is to encourage parents to live well while we're waiting to be reunited with our children in Heaven one day, bringing glory to God in the process. This goal of bringing bereaved parents together is accomplished primarily through our retreats.

We currently host three types of retreats for bereaved parents:
- Weekend-long retreats for couples/singles
- Weekend-long retreats just for dads
- One-day mini-retreats just for moms

At all of our events, we share our children's stories and discuss topics relevant to bereaved parents. We pray for each other and we encourage one another. We may shed some tears, but we also share in times of laughter as we discuss the hope we have in Jesus Christ. We may have many more years here on earth before we see our children again. Our desire is always to determine how we can live well "while we're waiting" to be reunited with our precious children in Heaven.

All of our events are offered at no charge to the attendees. A voluntary love offering is accepted at each event. We attained 501(c)(3) status in August of 2012, so all donations are tax deductible. No one receives any salary for their work with While We're Waiting, and all donations go straight to the operations of the ministry.

Our retreats are typically held in the Hot Springs, Arkansas, area, but we occasionally do events "on the road." We have hosted events in Picayune, Mississippi; Wichita Falls, Texas; Huntsville, Alabama; and other parts of Arkansas.

At the present time, we are using borrowed facilities for our retreats. However, we have seen the need to offer our While We're Waiting events more often due to the fact that they are filling up months in advance and we have waiting lists for all of them. Therefore, we are in the early stages of building our own retreat facility. Fifty acres in Hot Springs has been donated to the ministry, and this is where we are planning to build. The property is situated between two thoroughbred farms on the outskirts of the city, and is a beautiful site, with a pond and lots of mature trees. There is an older house on the property, which is being completely renovated. A large kitchen/dining area and ten hotel-style bedrooms will be added, so participants in our events will each have their own private bedroom and bath while they're staying with us. We have committed to building the While We're Waiting Refuge debt free, and we have faith that God will supply all that we need. We anticipate holding our first retreat at this location in October of 2016.

Registration for our events is through our website: www.whilewerewaiting.org.

In addition to our retreat events, we host two faith-based support groups just for bereaved parents in Arkansas. One meets on the last Wednesday night of each month at Hot Springs Baptist Church in Hot Springs, Arkansas, and the other meets on the second Wednesday night of each month at Cross Church in Springdale, Arkansas. One of our dreams is to have "While We're Waiting" chapters around the country. These would be support groups like those hosted by Compassionate Friends and Bereaved Parents USA, but with a basis in our faith in Jesus Christ as the one and only healer of broken hearts.

While We're Waiting hosts three Facebook groups. One is a public page, which can be found and followed by anyone by searching for "While We're Waiting." Another is a private page, with membership limited just to parents who have lost children. It can be found by searching for "While We're Waiting – Support for Bereaved Parents" and requesting to join. An encouraging quote or Scripture is posted daily on each of these pages, but the private page allows for conversation between parents who have experienced the death of a child. We also host a page just for bereaved siblings. It is also a private group, and can be found by searching for "While We're Waiting – Support for Bereaved Siblings" and requesting to join. A young pastor who lost his only sibling seven years ago is the moderator of that group.

The While We're Waiting Team loves to share their stories and the While We're Waiting ministry with churches and civic organizations.

For more information about While We're Waiting, please contact Jill Sullivan at jill@whilewerewaiting.org.

I tell you this, brothers: flesh and blood cannot inherit the kingdom of God, nor does the perishable inherit the imperishable. Behold! I tell you a mystery. We shall not all sleep, but we shall all be changed, in a moment, in the twinkling of an eye, at the last trumpet. For the trumpet will sound, and the dead will be raised imperishable, and we shall be changed. For this perishable body must put on the imperishable, and this mortal body must put on immortality. When the perishable puts on the imperishable, and the mortal puts on immortality, then shall come to pass the saying that is written:

"Death is swallowed up in victory."

"O death, where is your victory? O death, where is your sting?"

The sting of death is sin, and the power of sin is the law. But thanks be to God, who gives us the victory through our Lord Jesus Christ.

Therefore, my beloved brothers, be steadfast, immovable, always abounding in the work of the Lord, knowing that in the Lord your labor is not

1 Corinthians 15:51-58 | ESV

About the Author

Kathleen Duncan has been married to her husband Ron for 32 years. They met and married while attending the University of Oklahoma where Ron earned a degree in mechanical engineering and Kathleen earned an accounting degree. Kathleen is a Certified Public Accountant, but has been a stay-at-home wife and mom for the past 24 years, working only part-time during tax season.

Their seven children range in age from 20-31 - Margaret (Maggie), Peter, Andrew, Adam, David, Elizabeth (Lyz) and Meredith, who is married to Mark. Their children live in Texas, Oklahoma, Michigan, Tennessee, Georgia and Heaven.

Ron and Kathleen have lived in five states and now call fifteen acres in North Texas their home. When they first moved to Texas, they tried raising chickens but ended up with a few fat coyotes. They enjoy playing with their two dogs, a yellow lab named Lady and a fat, black pug named Lyla. They also enjoy watching the hawks, deer, turkeys and other wildlife from the back porch and riding their bikes. When Ron's work requires visiting customers (which is much of the time), Kathleen often joins him in his travels. They have visited forty-seven states in the past two years.

Ron and Kathleen educated all of their children at home. For fourteen years she taught Home School for High School seminars around the country helping home school families navigate high school and the college application process.

Kathleen's hobbies include reading, studying the Bible, swimming, biking and mowing their property. But her favorite hobby is visiting her grandchildren.

Contact the Author

kathleenbaileyduncan@gmail.com

To read more about

"My Journey through Grief into Grace",

visit her blog:

www.KathleenBDuncan.com

Or

"Like" her Facebook Page

Kathleen B. Duncan, My Journey through Grief into Grace

www.facebook.com/KathleenDuncanblog

Books by Kathleen Duncan

<u>My Journey through Grief into Grace</u>

Print Version
ISBN-13: 978-1516976638

EBook
Available on Amazon.com

<u>What Bereaved Parents Want You to Know</u>
<u>(but may not say)</u>

Print Version
ISBN-13: 978-1517528591

EBook
Available on Amazon.com

Made in the USA
San Bernardino, CA
08 November 2015